michae it's time

AP 02 '09

D1591962

ISBN 0-634-08168-3

HAL•LEONARD®
CORPORATION

7777 W. BLUEMOUND RD. P.O. BOX 13819 MILWAUKEE, WI 53213

Visit Hal Leonard Online at
www.halleonard.com

contents

FEELING GOOD

from THE ROAR OF THE GREASEPAINT - THE SMELL OF THE CROWD

Words and Music by LESLIE BRICUSSE
and ANTHONY NEWLEY

Slowly, freely

Birds fly-ing high, you know how I feel.

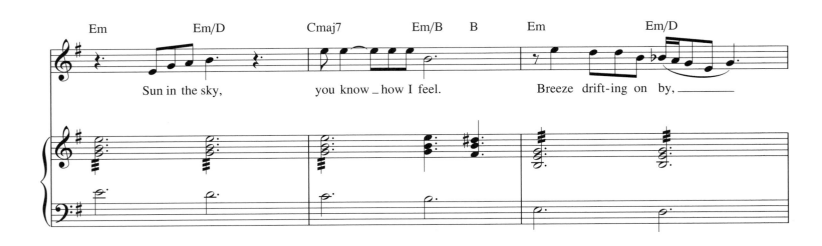

Sun in the sky, you know _ how I feel. Breeze drift-ing on by, _____

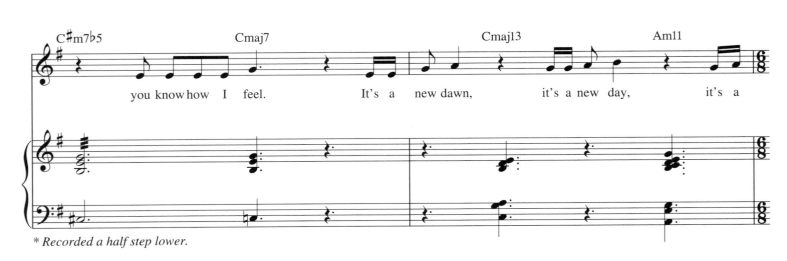

you know how I feel. It's a new dawn, it's a new day, it's a

* Recorded a half step lower.

6

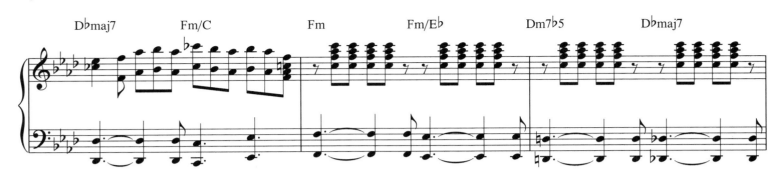

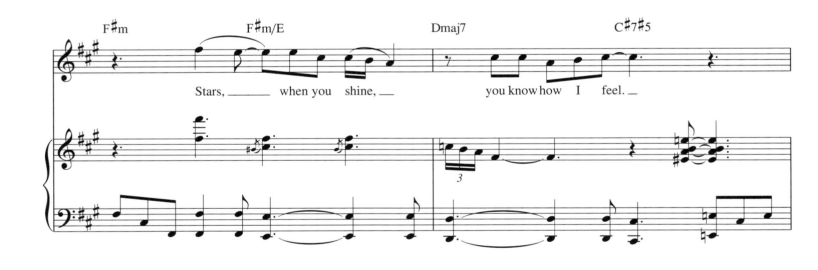

Stars, _____ when you shine, ___ you know how I feel. _

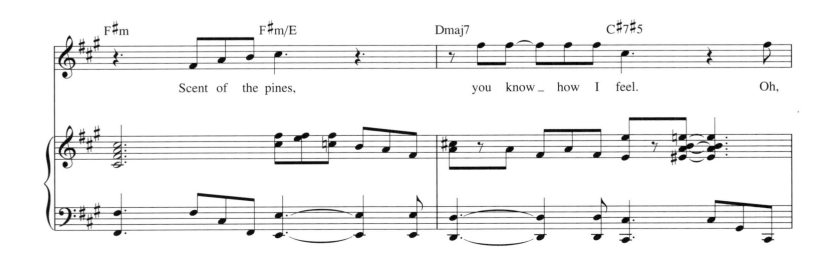

Scent of the pines, you know _ how I feel. Oh,

A FOGGY DAY

Music and Lyrics by GEORGE GERSHWIN
and IRA GERSHWIN

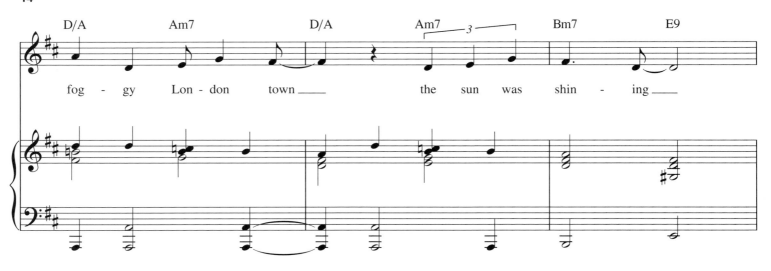

fog - gy Lon - don town _____ the sun was shin - ing _____

ev - 'ry - where. _____

YOU DON'T KNOW ME

Words and Music by CINDY WALKER
and EDDY ARNOLD

You give your hand to me and then you say hel-lo,
know the one who dreams of you at night
Guitar solo ad lib.
and I can
and longs to

hard-ly speak,
kiss your lips
my heart is beat-ing so. __
and longs to hold you tight. __
And an-y-
Ooh, __ I'm

one can tell
just a friend,
you think you know me well; __
that's all I've ev-er been, __
well, you don't
'cause you don't

QUANDO, QUANDO, QUANDO
(Tell Me When)

English Words by PAT BOONE
Italian Lyrics by A. TESTA
Music by TONY RENIS

Moderate Bossa

MALE: Tell me, when will you be mine?

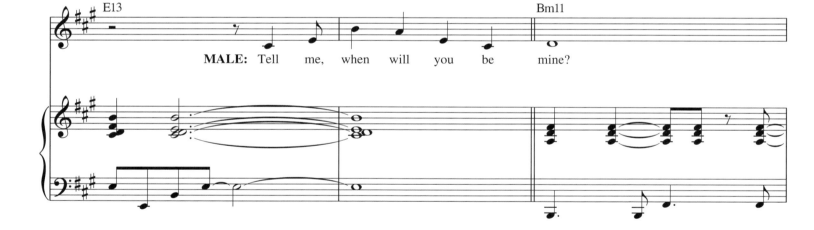

Tell me, quan-do, quan-do, quan-

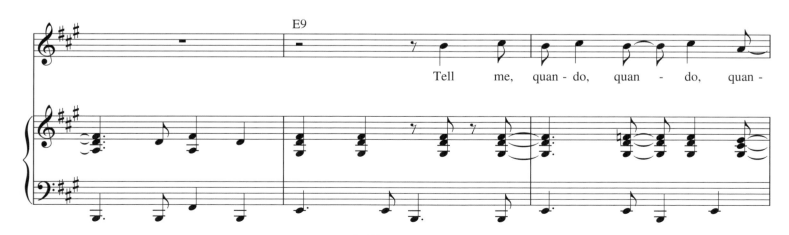

HOME

Words and Music by AMY FOSTER-GILLIES,
MICHAEL BUBLÉ and ALAN CHANG

Moderately slow

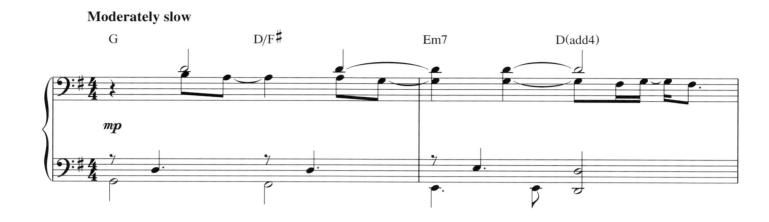

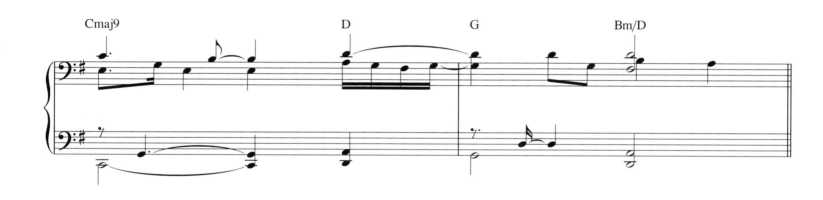

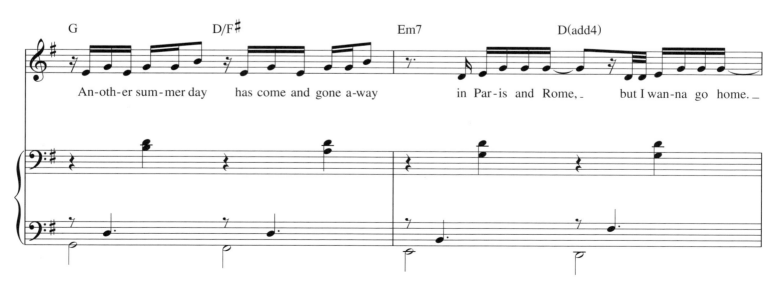

An-oth-er sum-mer day has come and gone a-way in Par-is and Rome,_ but I wan-na go home._

CAN'T BUY ME LOVE

Words and Music by JOHN LENNON
and PAUL McCARTNEY

(Play R.H. 2nd time only)

42

52

THE MORE I SEE YOU

Words by MACK GORDON
Music by HARRY WARREN

The more I see you,

56

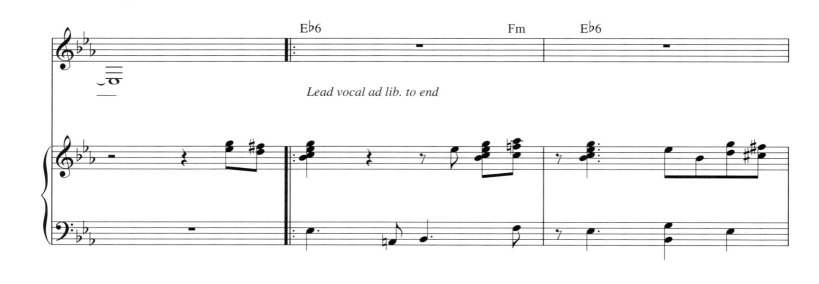

Lead vocal ad lib. to end

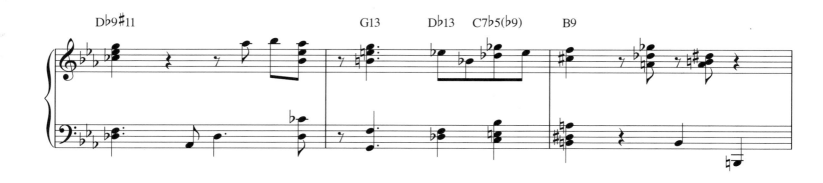

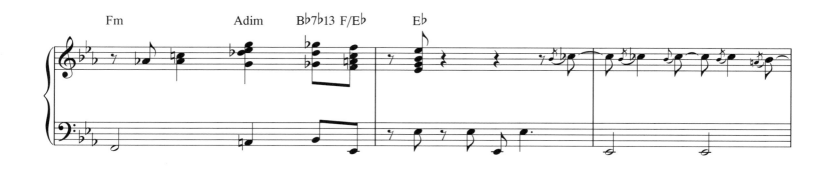

SAVE THE LAST DANCE FOR ME

Words and Music by DOC POMUS
and MORT SHUMAN

Moderate Latin beat

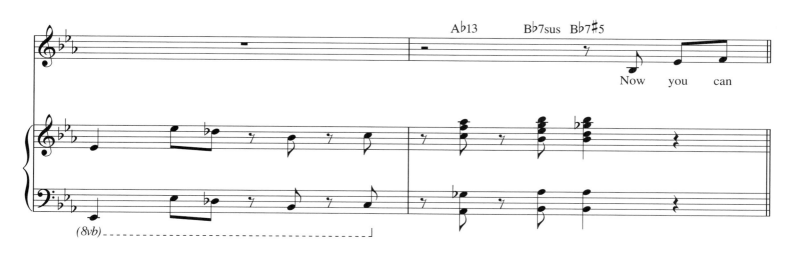

Now you can

dance   ev-'ry dance with a guy who   gives you the eye, _ let him
know   that the mu-sic's _ fine like   spar-kling _ wine. _ Go and

TRY A LITTLE TENDERNESS

Words and Music by HARRY WOODS,
JIMMY CAMPBELL and REG CONNELLY

75

HOW SWEET IT IS
(To Be Loved by You)

Words and Music by EDWARD HOLLAND,
LAMONT DOZIER and BRIAN HOLLAND

Need - ed the shel - ter of

some - one's arms, and there you were.

so man - y ways.__ I wan - na stop__ __ you.

A SONG FOR YOU

Words and Music by
LEON RUSSELL

Slowly

I've been so man-y plac-es in my life __ and time. __

I've sung a lot of songs; I've made some bad rhyme.

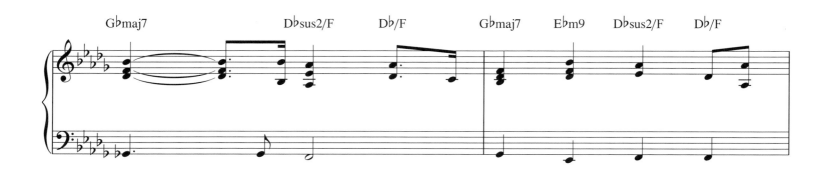

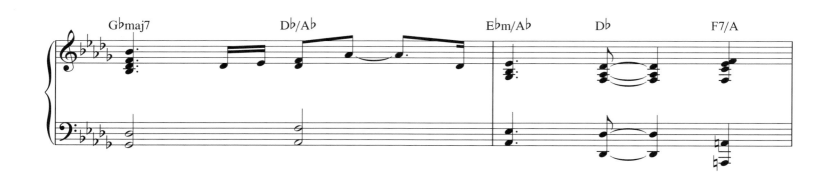

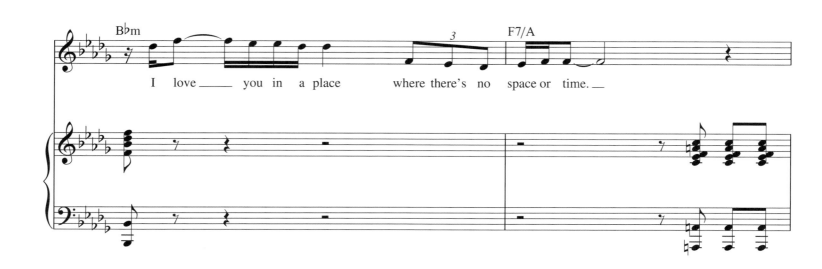

I love _____ you in a place where there's no space or time. _____

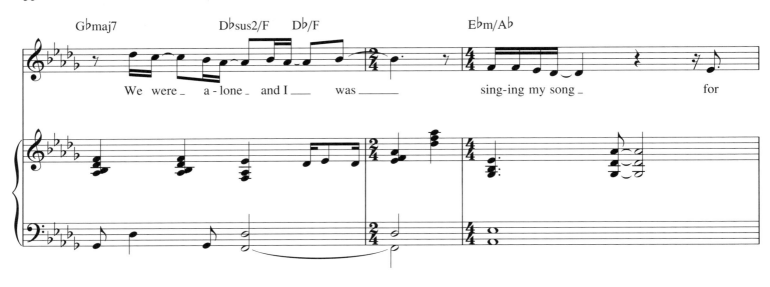

We were a-lone and I was sing-ing my song for

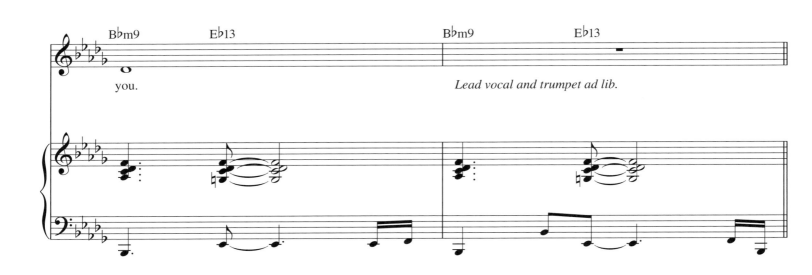

you.

Lead vocal and trumpet ad lib.

Play 4 times ad lib.

rit.

I'VE GOT YOU UNDER MY SKIN

from BORN TO DANCE

Words and Music by
COLE PORTER

stop, be - fore I be - gin, 'cause I've got you; __

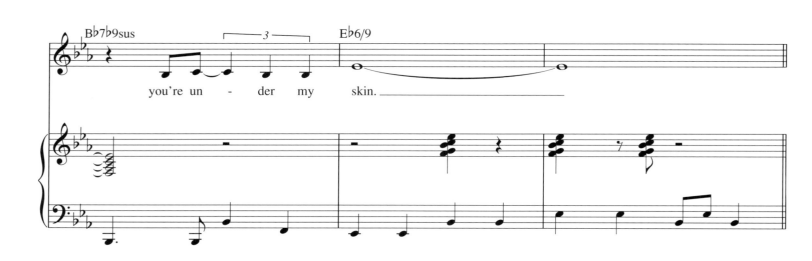

you're un - der my skin. __

Play 4 times

R.H. ad lib

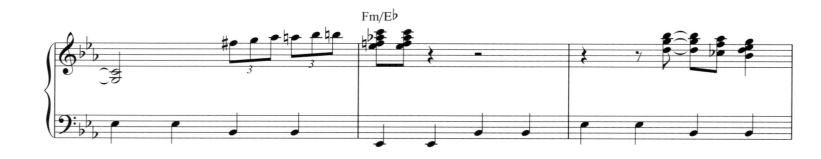

Fm/E♭

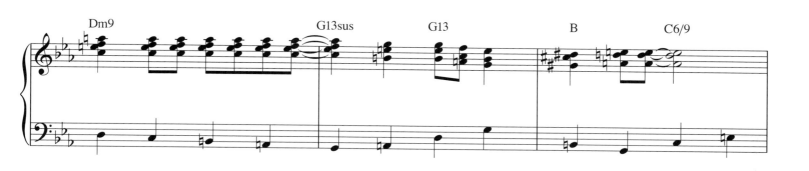

YOU AND I

99

Words and Music by
STEVIE WONDER

Slowly, freely

With pedal throughout

Here we are on earth to-geth-er. It's

you and I; God has made us fall in love. It's

true, I've real-ly found some-one like